The Leap,
and What You'll Reap

The Leap,
and What You'll Reap

From A Girl Who Wanted More

K. Glenn

Kindle Direct Publishing

Self-Publishing Assistance: C.L. Hodge
Book Cover Format: K. Glenn
Book Cover Creation: C. Sharp
Contributions: R. Glenn
Editing: K.S. Glenn, D. Thompson
Proofreading: K. Seymore, E. Glenn
Internal Text Format: K. Glenn
Beta Read: J. Newson

ISBN: 9781790587063

First giving honor to God,

to all of the people who helped me take a leap of faith:

my family, "The G-Team,"

my friends, for being consistent,

my mentees and little sisters, for keeping me on my toes,

my 1st class (the c/o 2018), for motivating me,

and to my best friend, Derrick, for constantly asking me "How long?" until this book was complete.

Thank you.

Contents

Preface

Immediately after finishing graduate school, I felt like I was on top of the world. I knew my professional years were approaching and it felt good to be "grown." Oh, how quickly this all changed once I started going to work every day. Whoa.

It dawned on me that what I was doing was not what I wanted to do for the rest of my life. Everyone says your twenties are the good years, the years when you have the time of your life and make all of these horrible, yet enjoyable, decisions. This wasn't entirely the case for me. I spent the beginning of these twenties trying to accomplish all of my academic goals, and as I started to approach my mid-twenties, I was unhappy with my day-to-day routine. Did I miss the hype? I wanted to be in the perfect city, with the perfect job, around all of my people. I know I'm not the only person who has reached this point.

Some of you have just graduated and realized you have no desire to use the degree you've worked so hard to obtain. Some of you probably dove head first into a line of work relevant to your degree, and then suddenly had a desire to switch as I did. Younger readers may be in college as we speak, but you're questioning whether or not you'll be able to finish because it's difficult to maintain and multitask. These feelings aren't limited to those with a college degree.

Maybe you've had an epiphany, for whatever reason, that you want to step out and do more with your life. Or, perhaps you want to do something different from what everyone in your family has done, but you're afraid to try because you're not sure who to look to for that blueprint you need. Regardless of who you are, when dissatisfaction hits you, it hits hard.

You are not alone.

This short, self-reflective body of work is the direct result of feeling unfulfilled where I was, being hungry for a new experience, and forcing myself to do something about it. I was about six months into a job search that was dry, draining, and difficult when I decided to start writing this. Out of all the applications I submitted, cover letters I edited, and resumes I reformatted, I only had three interviews. I was convinced something was wrong with me since nothing seemed to be coming through. I was waiting to hear back from the most recent interview I had for a university

I'd been eyeballing for quite some time. They told me they'd make their decision in a couple of weeks, after interviewing a few more candidates. Two weeks from that day, I sat by the phone anticipating a call for an offer. That call didn't happen.

At that point, I contemplated giving up. It was as if something clicked, and the unbothered façade I tried to preserve began to fade immediately. People warned me about resigning from one job before having something else lined up, but I did it anyway. I took the biggest leap of faith I'd ever made at that point in my life, and it felt like more of a mistake.

Did I tell anyone I felt this way? Absolutely not. I didn't want to hear any form of an "I told you so" or asked, "why don't you just _____?" You see, I wanted my next job to be in a city far from home for multiple reasons- Houston, Texas. I decided that I'd try to shoot my shot from

Tennessee because I refused to move before securing a position beforehand.

This was when life got real.

Suddenly, I found myself at a crossroads where any decision made would affect my professional and personal life (both being equally important). Getting these two to align felt like struggling to solve a Rubix cube and then abruptly putting it down when you've decided it's too complicated. The quest for a new job isn't as easy as people make it out to be, and I would argue the search itself is more work than the position you're vying for. My faith was put to the ultimate test.

The hardest thing about maintaining faith during difficult times is trying to discern every sign that you think you're getting. Why is this happening? Is this a sign to quit? Is this a sign to keep going? Is this a test to see how badly I want this? Was my leap of faith unwise? It all gets a little fuzzy in the thick of a major transition.

Now, in hindsight, I realize that I needed to stop clocking the process so that real growth could take place. I wasn't supposed to be able to pinpoint things, because I was supposed to be trusting God. What I was stressing about was actually giving me the tools I needed to grow and evolve as an individual before diving headfirst into new territory with new people.

I hope that while reading this small part of my story, you won't feel alone in this trying-to-find-your-passion phase of life. It's ugly, it's uncomfortable, and it forces you to learn hard lessons in some of the most inconvenient ways. If you can identify with anything that I've said thus far, I hope you finish this book feeling prepared, in some way, for what you will possibly face. I get it, and I'm right there with you- trust me.

I was in for a rude awakening.

SELF-APPLICATION | LAY IT OUT

(Oh, you thought you were just going to read?)

Write down the goal you've been putting off. If there is more than one, list them in order of priority before you begin reading.

_____

_____

_____

_____

_____

_____

_____

_____

_____

_____

_____

_____

_____

_____

_____

_____

_____

Phase I
Boarding

August 2014-February 2018

For as long as I can remember, I've always been a person who took pride in being overly prepared. Planning made me feel ready and able, and that gave me confidence.

When I was a competitive swimmer, I welcomed feedback from my coach to perfect my dive, flip turn, or time so I would snatch another medal at the next meet. As a violinist, I studied sheet music for playing tests weeks in advance to keep my seat as concertmaster in class. In college, especially if I knew there was an event approaching, I'd work tirelessly to complete any assignments as far ahead of the deadline as possible so I could play in peace. The same diligence was present in collaboration with other people. When acting, my scene partners and I practiced running through lines and blocking for our first collegiate play, *The Talented Tenth*, in front of our dorm room mirrors several times a week. We wanted our peers to be proud and, more importantly, upperclassmen to be impressed.

When I got ready to take a leap of faith from my first professional position, however, I didn't realize you can only plan to a certain extent. In hindsight, this leap was equivalent to preparing to catch a flight to another destination. You decide it's time to treat yourself to a getaway, put in a request to take off from work, and get ready to go. *Before* we take that flight, however, there are quite a few things we must take into consideration.

The first steps include making sure you've done all that you can to get onto the plane hassle-free. Can I consolidate my things into a carry-on, or will I check a bag? This will determine whether you'll need travel-sized toiletries or if you'll be able to take full-sized bottles. Is it better for me to catch a morning, afternoon, or an evening flight? This will determine what time you'll need to get to the airport and what time you'll arrive at your destination. Will I wear sandals to slip off at security, or find good socks so that I can wear tennis shoes? This will determine the speed at which you'll move through security. We sort each of these things out during the preplanning stage before each flight. Then, we think of being *on* the plane. Stay with me.

I am cold-natured, so a blanket is nonnegotiable. Between reading and watching movies, I prefer the latter on board. Now that I know this, I browse through the Netflix movies that are available for download and have these in place so I'm entertained for the duration of the trip. That's *more* planning to make sure the flight is as comfortable as possible. Do you see how we subconsciously pay attention to these details?

Thinking back to our very first flight, we were so unprepared and frazzled that we never want that to happen again- or at least I was. Now that we've adjusted, we have an idea of what's ahead even if we cannot predict how long the security line will be, if the weather will be agreeable, or even if the departure time will be delayed. We prepare, and then when the unexpected happens, it's a little easier to handle. This is how we must approach taking a leap of faith. I'll explain.

Teaching was not something I wanted to do for the rest of my life, and I knew this after my internship year during graduate school. The idea of working on a college campus piqued my curiosity after one of my summer jobs. Minority students seemed to struggle more with staying in college than actually getting there, and I wanted to help change that. Nevertheless, I was sure the likelihood of being hired in this field, straight out of college, was slim to none. It was after receiving my Master's degree that I began to "board."

Even though teaching was not the long-term goal, I knew it was imperative to take full advantage every available opportunity. By doing this, I could accumulate transferable skills for the next job. Swallowing this pill was not an easy thing to do. The need for quality educators, particularly in secondary education, is real. Many of the problematic issues that exist mirror things I witnessed and experienced in school and that alone could lead to another book (I'm tempted). Similar to being in a relationship with someone you know isn't "the one," however, I wasn't all the way there. The slightest mishaps felt like massive messes, and it was hard to appreciate the rewards that came with the profession fully. Here I was in a position to change lives around some of the brightest individuals, yet I wasn't completely happy. On top of this, I felt guilty for even wanting to leave and pursue my dream. I didn't want that desire to be misperceived as being ungrateful for the opportunities I'd been given.

I was torn.

Staying someplace where you are not wholeheartedly invested is tricky because the feelings you're working so hard to suppress will begin to bleed into your work, affecting your interactions with people. Despite how hard you try to act like it's all good, your actions will project a different story. If you're walking that fine line, it's time to make some adjustments. Once I realized I was approaching that line, I knew I needed to leave. My dream was to work on a college campus and everything done in the present was done with that in mind. It was time to move with purpose.

The first year, I only taught and observed. I listened to all of the people who rush to give first-year teachers the advice they may or may not need. During the second year, I wanted an opportunity to teach something that I was passionate about that didn't require adhering to guidelines set by the state.

As a result, I pitched an idea for an African American Literature elective course, and my Incomparable Curriculum Principal gave me the freedom to do so. During the third year, to generate enthusiasm and boost morale in my classroom, I reached out to First Lady Michelle Obama on behalf of my class and received a package as a response two months later. By the fourth year, I was not only a Dean but an evaluator as well. Test scores each year reflected substantial student growth. Despite all of this, I still felt unfulfilled.

The goals I set mattered to me, but they weren't milestone achievements for me personally. These were experiences I created for myself because I knew a time would come for me to take flight. I knew one day I was going to be on new territory, and I wanted to leave with a collection of skills and experiences that held weight. I want to think I did *at least* one thing each year to make the flight easier, knowing I couldn't predict how things would go once I was in the air.

The takeaway from that is this: before emotions drive you to abruptly quit whatever it is you're doing, stop and think with more logic. What can you do to maximize your experience(s) right where you are? What things can you add to your reservoir that will make "taking flight" a little easier? If you quit too soon, your experiences will be too limited to be even remotely prepared for what's next. Why? Because you need all the experiences a "less than ideal" job can offer now that you're there. That may sound strange but again, stay with me.

You need to have some people rub you the wrong way so you'll know how to handle it later (even if you didn't handle it well the first time...like me). You need to be able to pinpoint what it is you don't like, and why, so you're a little bit closer to knowing what it is you *do* want to do. You must make the best of **that** situation before venturing out onto what seems like greener grass because let's face it- there will always be some parts of working for someone else that you do not like. The Bible affirms making the most of things, too. Luke 16:10 reads,

"He that is faithful in that which is least is faithful also in much: and he that is unjust in the least is also unjust in much."

How you handle what's in front of you now will determine the quality of what's coming. I'm also convinced God purposely places us where we don't want to be because had we received what we wanted the first time we'd be arrogant. This is similar to how the media depicts some, but not all, child stars, although we don't see as many extremes as we used to. An adorable, charismatic kid is thrust into the spotlight too early, and as they enter their teenage years, there is great potential to be totally unprepared for fame.

The attention they're receiving can have an adverse effect on who they are, resulting in an entitlement mindset. Their difficulties could be numerous. They may turn to drugs. They may lash out. The paparazzi fuels this mindset, typically publishing some of the most unflattering candid photos in magazines to document their self-demise. As we can see, being unprepared has serious consequences. Anyone in a situation like this can quickly become egotistical, lacking substance. It's hard to like people who act this way, which brings me to my next point- You'll need references.

One of the most valuable pieces of advice I've ever received was from a boss who encouraged me to show more of my personality. At a young age, I was fortunate enough to have unique leadership opportunities in different capacities. Pressure to perform was a weight I always carried. Since I was young, I assumed my superiors would attribute any errors to my age, so I was a meticulous robot. I was so about "getting it done" that small talk was not all that appealing. Honestly, it made me uncomfortable.

It was more uncomfortable because I was a young, African American professional now working in culturally diverse settings with *new people*. I realized I was more at ease around my own for reasons many of you can understand. Around my own, I didn't feel like a spokesperson for my race. I didn't feel like I had to disguise my bad days to avoid being perceived as a "mad, Black woman." I didn't feel like I was around people who were trying to prove to me, whether they realized it or not, they weren't racist. If ever the outlier in a room, I felt it mandatory to be careful and calculated with my interactions so I was a respectable representative of African Americans, women, millennials, or all of the above. Anyone can relate to this feeling whether you're White or Hispanic, young or old, a man or a woman it doesn't matter. When you are the *only* person representing a group in any setting, it produces a pressure you can feel. All that to say, being around people who didn't look like me, on a daily basis, was a different ball game as an adult. Mingling was easier in college.

As comforting as being around my own felt, I knew I needed to find comfort in culturally diverse settings, too. When is the last time you got on a plane made up of people who look and act just like you? Furthermore, what makes you think that when you apply for the next job you won't be up against a diverse population? You must force yourself to grow in these ways, especially during today's times, to keep yourself well-versed, relatable, and sharp. You learn so much from other people and their cultures that *not* embracing them is only a disservice to yourself.

During the four years I was preparing to board, I wanted to make connections with new people and develop relationships as opposed to just being cordial (per the advice of my former boss). The problem was I had no idea how to do this. The first woman I ever trusted on a professional level, a petite powerhouse who I referred to as my "teacher mama," helped me out with this though I'm sure she didn't realize it.

When she walked in a room, you knew she meant business. She was a keen observer of all things, witty, and a team player. In many schools, first-year teachers are assigned a first-year mentor, and she was mine. Surprisingly, after only a few weeks, she made it clear I didn't need her assistance anymore, and she let me spread my wings. Although I was nervous about her cutting the cord as fast as she had, I appreciated her belief in me and, as a result, she became one of my first confidants and cheerleaders in the building. She broke the ice, and now being around people who didn't look like me wasn't so bad. I began warming up to others at my own pace, and when I was ready to take the leap and resign, I had a variety of people I could call on for references. These references were not only my friends, but could speak for me professionally.

What a difference a reference makes when they can attest to your character, personality, and work ethic, rather than merely saying, "Yea, she did her job well. Hard worker. Good results." New employers don't know you at all, so having a credible reference who can vouch for you being a well-rounded candidate is crucial.

The idea that we can maneuver through this world on our own strength, with no support whatsoever, is an egregious one. You need people. Rather than using them for what they have, or dismissing them because of one characteristic you may not like, take the time to bond with those who show themselves trustworthy. You'll learn from each other's strengths and weaknesses, only strengthening that working relationship while you're there.

I had the opportunity to work with different types of personalities, collaborate with four women I admired, act as a positive role model for students, and learn many lessons that could only help me in future endeavors. Closing the door on one chapter of your life isn't so bad when you *know* you made the most of your time there. Boarding is the easy part.

Now, it's time for takeoff. Ready?

SELF-APPLICATION | BOARDING

Think briefly about at least three things that you
can do at your current job, or in your current
circumstance, to maximize your time there.

_____

_____

_____

_____

_____

_____

_____

_____

_____

_____

_____

_____

_____

_____

_____

_____

_____

_____

_____

_____

SELF-APPLICATION | BOARDING II

Proverb 27:17 reads, "Iron sharpeneth iron; so a man sharpeneth the countenance of his friend." Think of 2-3 people with whom you would like to have a better relationship with + why.

_____

_____

_____

_____

_____

_____

_____

_____

_____

_____

_____

_____

_____

_____

_____

_____

_____

_____

Phase II
Takeoff

May 2018

How frustrating is it to be seated and comfortable on the plane, and then hear the captain announce that there will be a delay? We're like, "Whew chile; we're ready to go!" I didn't get all of my luggage together, get up early, rush here, buy food, bring the blanket, and get my movies ready to sit here. I have somewhere to go, sir! This is what's beautiful about making a personal or professional shift. Once you've prepared, the only person responsible for any delay is you.

Or who you have around you.

One of the most uncomfortable things about working with people, in general, is the inevitability of being around complacent individuals. The undertones of your conversations with them are inherently negative regardless of how positive you try to be. These people exist regardless of the career you're in, the school you attend, or the organization you're connected to, so there's no dodging them. Pessimism of this nature befuddles me.

If you feel your voice is never heard, then why not speak up? If you're unhappy with what you're doing, why not do something different? If you're struggling, why not ask for help? If someone offended you, why not address it if you know you'll have to be around them? If you feel overlooked, why not do something to be…seen? I didn't get it. Until one day I did.

When it comes to older peers, it's not easy for those who have children and spouses to move as freely as they wish because they have a greater responsibility to their families. While I was young and free, they were knee deep into another stage of life I'd not yet approached. Any and every decision they made affected multiple people, and because of this, it limited what they were able to do. Job security was a priority, not following their hearts and finding happiness.

I'm sure this is why some people looked at me like I was crazy when I went on a slight tangent about my desire to make a change. When I'm passionate about a subject, I want all things fixed and implemented instantly. It's like wanting your mom to buy that pair of shoes in the store the day you see them, but she tells you she'll think about it. You know they'll be gone if she decides to go back. I received the courtesy smile and nod that read more like "Bless her heart" or the classic "Good luck with that!" It was almost as if I could tell they didn't believe in my dreams, but it wasn't that. They didn't have time to dream. Here is where you must protect your space at all costs.

While it was not my place to look at them differently for not thinking the way I did, that didn't mean I had to downsize my ideas and make their excuses my excuses. When they projected fear or worry, I needed to shield myself from absorbing those projections. If you do not shield yourself, the skeptical glances and doubtful exchanges can, and will, rub off on you.

When you are working, or in school, you are around your peers for a majority of the day, for a majority of each week, all year. This means any negativity around you can and will permeate your spirit whether you're aware it's happening or not. You'll be upset when there's no reason to be angry. You'll question yourself when you were initially confident. If you allow them, toxic people will run your life.

Once you've been infected, your belief in flight will be watered down by the doubts of those who have issues irrelevant to you. You, too, will begin making excuses for why you can't and won't pursue that "thing." I remember one day while I was talking to my boyfriend during one of our routine FaceTime dates, he called me out on this. It was another day when I got home later than planned, and I was irritable. I was hungry, too. Normally he didn't mind listening to the typical "I had a bad day" spiel, but on this day he must have had enough of this because his response to my work rant took me by surprise.

"You're starting to sound like the people you talk about," he responded.

Excuse me? How dare he make such a comparison? The nerve. He's supposed to be telling me it'll be okay, that this will all pay off, and that I'm the bomb. Should we break up and be friends? I don't like this.

"You just sat here and complained for like 20 minutes, talking about that same stuff you've *been* talking about for a while. What's the point?"

Wow. He basically just told me to shut up. His response aggravated me a little bit, too. He said this while eating dinner, compliments of room service, in his luxury hotel room courtesy of the company he worked for at the time. He didn't do what I did, so what did he know anyway, right? Wrong. Reluctantly, though I didn't *want* to hear what he said, I had to admit he was right (and I'm sure he loves this statement being in writing).

For a moment I almost let a small number of people rub off on me and get me off kilter. I couldn't concede to the current circumstances and delay my own flight. Sometimes, we need that reality check from the people who are closest to us whether it feels good or not. If they can't tell us to get it together, then who can? I guess the idea of breaking up was a slightly dramatic but hey, we all have our days.

I also realized some were indifferent simply because they were comfortable. Contentment is a state of mind we all should aim to embody, but being *too* comfortable is dangerous.

It's easy to be "the man/woman" in one spot, at one job, or in one city. When we walk into a room where people know our name and can vouch for our abilities, it feels like we are where we're supposed to be. Recognition is something we all appreciate. Walking into a room where no one knows you is what's challenging. You're essentially rebuilding your name from the ground up and that takes work.

Being the big man on campus at your high school is one thing, but when you go to college can you do it all over again among thousands of students? Being a hometown hero is cool, but can you go somewhere else and gain the same respect? The idea of stepping out takes a certain level of humility everyone doesn't want to accept, but to move to higher ground, this is a skill we must master. If you don't accept this, your plane will never leave the ramp. You will be sitting idly by, wasting time in your prideful bubble, livid that everyone else is moving ahead because you feel you're more equipped than they are.

"Who does he think he is?"

"Why'd they chose *her*?"

"I could've done that; I just didn't want to."

Get over yourself.

Old glory stories lose their appeal over time, and "shoulda coulda woulda" statements are unproductive. What are you doing *right now*? You've done so much talking, had so many dreams, and laid out so many plans. Now, it's time to do something about it. As aggravated as we are when the captain announces a delay, is just how aggravated you'll be with yourself if you keep making excuses for why you should deal with things you don't *have* to deal with. I watched a Tupac Shakur interview on YouTube loosely related to this.

I always enjoy watching his commentary on the state of America as it pertains to the less fortunate, but in this particular interview, he made a statement that resonated with me. He mentioned never seeing any "loud mouth thirty-year-olds." In saying this, he was referring to the fight for justice and equality and how, as people age, their passion for these concepts die because of the constant resistance to positive change. This, I understood, is why it is imperative to invest in younger generations because they will always be the heart of major movements. This type of burn out impacts personal and professional aspirations, too.

When most people reach a certain level or age, they stop aspiring because they're exhausted. They've decided to be content with the progress they've made and coast from there. I don't want to coast. If you're reading this book, I know you don't want to coast either. *We* want to make something shake. So, if we have everything we need to pursue the next level, to leap, to take flight, then why would we back out? There is no logical answer, aside from money. But this doesn't *have* to be a reason.

Once I said goodbye to my job, I knew I needed to have money to carry me through the unexpected. As free-spirited as I can be, I'm not naïve. I did a little research and discovered the average time it takes to find a job is six months. That's a huge chunk of the year!

That's a long time to be unemployed whether you've recently graduated from college, want to switch careers, or are trying to launch your own thing. If I wasn't employed before my benefits expired, I knew I would need to pay health insurance out of pocket. I also needed to be able to catch a flight if an interview presented itself, gas to get around in the meantime, and money to eat. Here is where I began to be frugal, and here is another flight analogy.

Once you're in the air, you're not able to use your phone, Wi-Fi isn't an option unless you're willing to pay, and you can only get out of your seat when the pilot signals that it's safe to do so. Your only options are to read a book, watch those pre-downloaded movies on your device, take advantage of the free channels they offer, or go to sleep. Once you say goodbye to one situation and take a leap of faith, you're limited like this as well. You'll need to prepare for this new normal even though it is temporary. It's time to cut back.

I started looking for things to cut out of the equation for the time being. My substitute for Apple music was Spotify's free streaming option. I listen to music every day, so finding a free streaming alternative wasn't an option (the ads weren't so bad). Rather than depending on Netflix, I watched many of my old DVDs. Used bookstores offer something like two dollars for fifty DVDs anyway, so I'm glad I decided to hold on to them. I even stopped eating out as much and ate things like oatmeal for breakfast, so I was full for a more extended period of time.

When invited to certain trips and outings, I had to be a big girl and decline despite how badly I wanted to indulge. My money needed to be self-managed in a strategic way because I didn't know how long it'd need to stretch. While I didn't enjoy saying "no," I needed to be real with myself. You can't keep "doing it for the 'gram" when you're trying to become a better version of who you are. For those who don't understand the "gram" reference, I'll gladly explain.

Social media moves us to take pictures, record videos, and give updates on our mobile app of choice. In an effort to capture every moment, constant documentation is indeed the latest trend. Although I'm not as hooked on it as others are, I do indulge every now and then. You tell people where you're going, show them what you're wearing, and display all of the good food you're eating. A 'like' or 'comment' on a picture is almost equivalent to receiving a compliment in person. Everyone loves a compliment.

Photo and video filters are good for making your life look "lit," even if it's an altered perception of your reality. It's like screaming, "Look at me! Look at what I'm doing! Look!" A lot of people try to act like they're unaffected by this, but I don't buy it. When cell phones started evolving into Smartphones, we all got into it. When television streaming developed, we were all looking for the perfect streaming device. Social media isn't any different. We're all pretty much into it at this point. When you take a leap of faith, there isn't much to capture that looks "lit," and that's when I noticed something.

When I posted on social media, I seemed to speak to people on a regular basis. You post a picture, and they comment. You upload a video, and they direct message you. You write a new status, and they share it (the list goes on). Oddly enough, when I stopped posting, I stopped hearing from people as much. This was something I hadn't expected, or planned for, because social media shouldn't matter that much, right? But social media can teach you some hard lessons, too. This, in combination with other dynamics, is when things got a pretty rocky.

"Ladies and gentlemen, the Captain has turned on the fasten seatbelt sign. We're experiencing some unexpected turbulence right now. Please remain in your seat until the Captain signals otherwise.

Thank you"

Buckle up, because it's about to get real.

Think of the excuses you've created to justify putting off your leap of faith. Write them out, and then explain why these are no longer valid.

_____

_____

_____

_____

_____

_____

_____

_____

_____

_____

_____

_____

_____

_____

_____

_____

_____

_____

Choose at least three things to eliminate for the sake of financial efficiency. If possible, list alternatives that could temporarily suffice.

_____

_____

_____

_____

_____

_____

_____

_____

_____

_____

_____

_____

_____

_____

_____

_____

_____

_____

_____

Phase III
Turbulent Weather

July 2018

You've planned your trip, boarded the plane, taken off, and then the inevitable happens—All of the ugly stuff for which you were totally unprepared.

If you've been on a turbulent flight, you know no matter how hard you try to ignore the fact that you're swaying from side to side, thousands of miles in the air, you can't. When you look around, you'll notice four types of passengers during such a flight. First, you have the passenger who isn't reacting at all. Your immediate thought is, "Do you not feel this?!" and you find their demeanor unusual. The second passenger is the overreacting kind. They're doing the absolute most, and you want them to stop because you're sure the panic will become infectious. Sleeping passengers are the third, and although you're somewhat jealous because you wish you were knocked out as well, you don't understand how they're unmoved by the obvious commotion. Finally, there are the passengers who are looking around just like you are. You meet eyes for a moment and quickly look elsewhere because their anxiety is just as loud as yours. None of these passengers make you feel better. Welcome to the unemployed life-where you look around, and nothing feels comforting.

The first thing I noticed when I looked around is that people are nosey. This isn't anything you realize until you've had someone ask you a question you don't want to answer, yet you're being *pressed* for the answer. What was difficult for me was knowing I'd leave January of

2018, but wanting that decision to remain under the radar. Applications would ask if current employers could be contacted and I would always select no. I didn't want word to spread-especially since I hadn't planned everything out yet. Planning was turning into my Achilles' heel.

Resigning was even more real when I told my apartment complex I would not be renewing my lease and filled out paperwork confirming my move out date. I did this to force myself into taking real action, or I'd be locked into another school year. It's like saving a flight online, but not checking out. You're not going anywhere until you click **purchase**.

I finally resigned during the summer and immediately afterward, I was hit with countless questions from several people around me. It's like being grilled by your family at holiday functions about school, life, and your "little friend," when all you want to do is eat in peace and play spades. Deflection is your new forte.

One assumption was "She must be engaged!" and I was asked about the progress of my relationship, one of the most intrusive topics you can inquire about. Keeping my personal life private was, and still is, important to me. Giving too many people too much access can create a conflict of interest, and I refused to open that can of worms, but I digress. I was asked where I was going. If I didn't give a straight answer, one or two would send someone else to ask me (to see if they received a more detailed response). It was a lot.

I was not necessarily wished well or told I'd be missed as quickly as I was asked, "Well, what's next?" It was almost as if people assumed I didn't have a plan since I wasn't laying it out for them to dissect and analyze. I hated this. Here's a word for whoever is reading this who is guilty of one of the things mentioned above …

People will tell you what they want you to know.

If you're completely engrossed in what someone else has going on with their life, you should probably find more things to occupy your own time. Such a heightened level of interest is, quite frankly, unhealthy. Someone else's life owes you no explanation, and no one is obligated to share the details of their personal plan with you- regardless of who you are. And why push the subject if it's clear they don't want to discuss it? Why some people feel entitled to know what is going on in everyone else's world is mindboggling to me. You may have advice to offer, and it may very well be sound and sensible, but refrain from offering it to someone who didn't ask. If you're offended they won't appease you in this, ask yourself why. What's it to you anyway? It's already uncomfortable to be unsure about what's next without being given the third degree.

For me, it was easy to dodge some of the questions that may have come from colleagues because I packed up my things, with the help of my guy, the day after the 4th of July. It worked. I exited in a manner that would ensure my peace of mind. The custodian made this even easier with helping hands and a sincere, "I'll miss ya, Glenn." I was packing, reality was setting in, and I was a little emotional. My mind was running a mile a minute; I couldn't handle any more inquiries.

After that, I looked around again and had to accept the fact that I was back home. My upbringing was fine, and I didn't grow up with a horrible home life by any means, but moving home after being independent for multiple years is a whole new world. I felt defeated. Fun fact: I never want to feel like a burden to other people (even though I know my family didn't feel this way). I will reciprocate things as quickly as I can so people know I'm not one to take advantage, but now I wasn't in a position to do so. That's rough, especially considering the amount of time

I spent in my own company. Everybody was at work, and that left me trying to figure out how to utilize all of this newfound free time. This is where things may get rough for you, too.

Initially, this alone time was somewhat refreshing because I had the opportunity to process the enormous transition I made by making the big leap, quitting my job, and planning for what was next. I moved in with my sister with the idea that it would be a two-months-max type of thing, and it was all good. After a few weeks, I noticed that every time she came in from work I was sitting on the same spot on the couch, having been nowhere that day. I'd wake up, apply to a few jobs, follow up with old applications, and then watch television. As a few of my friends would say, I became disgusted with myself.

When I got off of work, I remember how good it felt to come home and have time to decompress alone. My guy and I created a rule for this, too. We gave each other at least an hour after getting off work to unwind before talking to each other. We need an opportunity to shake the day, especially if it's a rough one, so we don't come to blows. Yet here I was, a couch potato my sister saw every time she walked around the corner once she got home. I felt like Felicia from the movie *Friday*. It was time to add some things to my daily routine.

Outdoor running is my exercise of choice, and I decided to begin two-a-days since I had the time. I ran around noon, and again around five o' clock so my sister had the house to herself when she got home from work or travels. I began investing a new piece of clothing into my wardrobe every couple of weeks so when I did get a job, my attire was on point. I added daily Bible readings. Traveling to meet with recruiters and prospective employers became routine, too. Once I got the hang of this, a friend of mine texted me with some exciting news.

"Hey, girl! Are you interested in going on a service trip to Haiti?!

While visiting one friend in Charlotte, North Carolina, I made a new friend, Jasmine. We exchanged contact information because we were both traveling out of the country that year- Jasmine to Morocco and me to Italy. Had it not been for this divine connection, I would've missed out on the incredible opportunity that was about to present itself. We met for a reason.

A final spot opened up for a service trip to Haiti, a collaboration between ATL4Haiti and Jasmine's organization Destination Impact (both based in Atlanta, Georgia). Meagan, the CEO of ATL4Haiti, was passionate about rounding up a group of people to give back to the Mission of Grace organization there in Carries.

Jasmine would always keep me in the loop about Destination Impact trips, but I wasn't comfortable taking off from work multiple times a week during the school year. I didn't have an excuse this time. Although this dipped into what I'd allotted for my unemployed savings, I knew it'd be worth the dip. Giving back to those in need is a great way to spend any free time you may have. Those seven days of service in Carries were *life-changing.*

A bonus was meeting seven people and developing friendships with them after the trip. We call ourselves "The Great 8" and we gas each other up on a regular basis in our group text because that's what friends do. If you can find a service trip to participate in while you're unemployed- do it. Being in a developing country is an excellent way to keep your spirit in check and meet new people. If an abroad excursion it too much, look at opportunities right there in the city where you reside. Opportunities to serve are everywhere, and if you can't find any, you can create them (the way Meagan did).

All of these things made those first few months home easier to manage. It was the months after that service trip that started to ruffle my feathers because, deep down, I thought I was the exception to the six-month average job search. I was only supposed to be home for two months…max.

■ ■

When I took the time to look around again, I noticed that notifications on my phone were pretty much nonexistent, aside from frequent rejection emails I received from different jobs I applied to since resigning. It felt like nobody noticed the fact that I pulled all the way back from everything. I know somebody out there has had the thought, "Would we be friends if I didn't ____?" or "Why do *I* always have to reach out first?" That's how I felt at the time.

When you are low key, you're officially out of sight and out of mind. If you've ever noticed this, it doesn't necessarily feel good. It feels silly to admit since you know people are just "living their lives," but we can't deny being human. On top of that, there were a couple of instances where my friends actually became mad at me. Yep, you read that right. I was going through something, and they were upset. Their feelings, oddly enough, were valid.

See, there are different types of friends. There are the friends who will be down for a trip without hesitation, there are those who you call when you need a pick me up because they know just what to say, and then there are those who always check in with you and initiate contact. There are more than this, but you get my drift. I was the check-in friend. It was nothing to tag my friends in funny Instagram videos, text a funny meme, call to talk about nothing, or even text a simple "have a good day" message or an "I'm thankful for you, girl" text around the holidays. What happened when this stopped? People got pretty confused.

When people have grown accustomed to you being a certain way, and you deviate from that, this doesn't sit well with them, but if you think about it, that's unreasonable. Are people not supposed to grow and evolve? If you were mean and you decide you want to be more kind, they're skeptical. You're *too nice*. If you were naïve and began to wise up, they could be upset because the new you doesn't vibe well with old them. You're *acting funny*. It's lose-lose.

On a couple of occasions, when people didn't "hear from me," they felt like there was some sort of unspoken issue. If someone hit me up to talk and I wasn't my usual self, they may have assumed I didn't want to talk to them, but this wasn't true. In reality, I needed someone to talk to—I just wasn't in a good place. Every thought that crossed my mind during those hours alone in the house became overpowering. It was like having an angel on one shoulder, and a devil on the other. I was always looking back and forth.

Ya girl had whiplash.

When we're going through things, we're not always able to articulate what space we're in at the time. Having just returned from service work in Haiti, I struggled with opening up to people even more. Although what I was dealing with was all the way real for me, it seemed microscopic compared to what I knew other people were dealing with in the world. I'm crying about employment, but I know of kids who are racing one another down rocky roads barefoot because they can't afford decent shoes. I'm sad about being home, but the home I'm in has air and heat while many homes in the world have no modern luxuries.

You want to be heard, but you don't have anything to say. You want to vent, but you don't want to feel like you're bogging someone else down with your issues. You want somebody to ask you how you're doing, but you're afraid to be honest about how you're *really* doing because being vulnerable like that is...eh. You realize you're projecting negative energy, but you don't know what to do about it at the moment. You're a conundrum. All you want is a friend who gets it and what's puzzling is you probably have several who do. We all experience the same lessons in different ways, but we hardly share. Why?

While in Haiti, we ate every meal together like one big happy family. One day at the table, one of the ladies initiated an exercise where someone gives you a word, any word, and you create a life principle out of it. This was when I realized I'm an ambivert. I love gatherings and being around people, but whenever somebody says, "Let's go around the room and everyone…" Whew! I want to get up and go to the bathroom, or take a fake phone call, and come back when I know they've gone all the way around *without me*. Unfortunately, I'd already gone to the bathroom when someone suggested this activity.

We didn't have cell phone service either. It was my turn.

The guy sitting across the table from me, a barber who came on the trip to give free haircuts to young boys in the village, assigned me the word chapter. The irony. Everyone reacted like, "Oh yeah that's a good one!" and "Dang, I wish I had that word!" This made me feel even more nervous because now there was pressure to say something *really* good. I sat there silently for about a minute and a half, which is a long time when people are just looking at you. Finally, I came up with a principle I thought could fit.

"When we read books," I started slowly, "the most interesting parts are the parts with the most action, conflict, and/or drama. This is the case for movies, too."

I stopped and looked around. Everyone was listening to me so attentively that I wanted to be careful with my words. I was one of the last to do this activity, and everybody who'd gone before me had such profound principles I wanted to keep the bar high. I looked down as I continued as if visualizing what I was trying to say on the table.

"Ironically, in real life, when we're actually in one of those challenging chapters, we are reluctant to share the details, but we should. Because...well, those are the chapters that bless others the most. Okay, I'm done." I looked up.

"Yasssss, that was deep!" they all exclaimed.

"OKAY, PRINCIPLE! COME THROUGH, LIFE LESSON! LET'S GO, WISDOM!"

Seriously, doesn't it feel good to be gassed up from time to time? Once it was out of my mouth, I started smiling to myself and thought about what I just said. That was a word for me, from me! It hit me then that being open is how people are healed. Nobody discusses their lows to the same extent they discuss their triumphs. I respect this because, as mentioned earlier, nobody is obligated to share the details of what's going on with them. While this is true, once we've come through a turbulent time, we shouldn't underestimate the beauty of our testimonies.

Healing happens when we know we're not alone and know there is a brighter side to our issues. This is true for anybody: victims of abuse, those who may struggle with fertility, people dealing with a painful breakup, those trying to break family cycles, students in college…it doesn't matter. Being understood is refreshing.

We appreciate knowing somebody has been up against what we're currently battling and prevailed. Any time we choose not to share some of our lows, we inadvertently miss the opportunity to be a calming force during somebody else's turbulence. I realized the reason I was struggling the way I was, was because I did keep so much to myself. I rarely shared anything and, as a result, I was getting in my own way.

We've got to do better.

Finally, as I looked around one more time, during all of this jobless rocky ridiculousness, I noticed one last thing that didn't help. Everyone had things to celebrate. While I'd pulled back from actually posting stuff on social media, I lurked on a regular basis because...well, I had the time. Don't judge.

People were living their best lives in high definition: being engaged, getting married, having beautiful babies, landing big shot jobs, traveling the globe just because, eating gourmet food on pretty plates...you name it; it was happening. Now listen, I'm hype when I see people flourish, especially people I know and love. I just wanted to be able to relate. I wanted "lit pics!" I wanted to make moves! I wanted to have something of my own to be proud of just as they did.

At this point, I was so enthralled with what everyone else had going on I couldn't fuel self-empowerment because I was wallowing in self-doubt. What was in front of me almost made me forget what Galatians 6:9 encourages us to do when it says, *"And let us not be weary in well doing: for in due season we shall reap, if we faint not."* Shall means will, and this is a definitive statement. I *will* receive what I've been praying and working for.

I was courageous enough to take a leap of faith, and I was consistently knocking on doors, so there was no reason to be dispirited. What I saw on social media could have been the result of a leap of faith these people took months or even years ago. Likewise, their celebrations weren't an indication that I was doing anything wrong. We're all in different lanes. It was time to eliminate distractions from my peripheral view and take a break from social media.

After a few final scrolls, I deleted any and every social app you can think of from my phone and tablet. The first few days were tough. You don't realize how much you use something until you're not using it anymore, similar to going on a diet. You say to yourself, "Okay, I'm not going to eat anything starchy this month." When you go grocery shopping, you realize that starch is in chips, bread, pasta, corn, rice, cereal...fries?! Okay, what is there left for me to eat? Once you're over the initial hump of change- maintaining discipline is easy.

These eliminations helped me examine who I am, what my strengths and weaknesses are, and how I needed to move forward with my search for a new job without distractions. Only then, after I stopped looking at everyone else, did the turbulence begin to diminish. After all, some of it was self-inflicted, but when you know better, you do better.

The hardest part is over and look at you,

You're just fine.

Now that you know you'll have some time to fill, here's an opportunity to plan for it. What are some things you can do while you wait on God to open your predestined door?

_____

_____

_____

_____

_____

_____

_____

_____

_____

_____

_____

_____

_____

_____

_____

_____

_____

_____

Let's take it a step further. What are some opportunities you can <u>create</u> for yourself? Start a business? Pursue music? Write a book? Create a club/group? Flush out the details below.

_____

_____

_____

_____

_____

_____

_____

_____

_____

_____

_____

_____

_____

_____

_____

_____

_____

Phase IV
Preparing to Descend

November 2018

When the captain announces that we are about to land and gives us an approximate time until we arrive at the gate, we're relieved. Everyone re-adjusts in their seats, fixes their hair, throws away trash, and prepares to get up and exit the aircraft. For some, this getting off point is a little overwhelming because everyone stands up almost instantly (like that's going to make them get off of the plane any faster). Some will even try to squeeze by you from their window seat to get their luggage from the overhead bin before the door has even opened. Those who remain seated find this a little amusing. What's the rush?

They know their best bet is to be patient and go with the flow because trying to be the first one in the aisle won't make you the first one off of the plane. This is what happens in real life once we've weathered the storm. Once we've gotten through turbulence, we can smile at any chaos around us because we are finally centered in ourselves. We are all going to end up where we're supposed to be. What's meant for us isn't going *anywhere*.

There was a point where I applied to so many jobs I knew I needed to fall back from this, too. Whenever I would check postings online, there were none left which made sense because the end of the year was approaching. That was when I became adamant about finishing this book. I wanted to capture every feeling in real time so it would resonate with those who are in the middle of their own transitional period, and prepare those who are about to be there. It was time to let go of the obsession I had with figuring out what was keeping me from landing a new position. Sometimes we all need to loosen our grips.

Stop crying.

Stop fighting.

Stop questioning.

And be still.

Every desire that's on your heart didn't get there on its own. It's not anything you thought up one day from some "aha" moment you had alone in your room. God strategically placed it there. This desire is your unique identifier in this world because there is nobody out there with your story, who has that desire. When He placed this on your heart, He also gave you the ability to fulfill that desire whether you realize it or not.

You already have everything you need to make something shake and get through tumultuous times. He'll even see to it that your greatest flaw works in your favor. There is nothing wrong with you.

This phase is one of the shortest because it's when you shake things off and accept the discomfort of where you are. You've come too far to turn back. I couldn't call my old job up and say, "Aye! Can I get that job back?" How can you fully work towards the future with the idea of backtracking lurking in your mind? **Faith and doubt cannot, and were never intended to, coexist. You must pick one.**

Know that even though there may not be any immediate movement when you take your own leap of faith, you're doing more than some people are willing to do when they're unhappy. You could've remained complacent, you could've wasted time, and you could've quit back when turbulence had you swaying from side to side thousands of miles in the air. You should be proud of your bravery because when the thought of quitting crossed your mind you could've interpreted that as a sign to renege, and you didn't.

I finally felt ready to shake everything off and start being a better version of myself. The thought of being out and someone asking me, "Hey what have you been up to?" used to give me anxiety, but not anymore. I wonder, now, how God feels when we step out on faith but then keep it to ourselves as if we're ashamed of trusting Him out loud. I knew it was time to stand up, stretch it out a little bit, and get off of the aircraft. I'd been in the air, and in my head, for way too long.

It is what it is.

What are some things you are proud to have accomplished so far? It doesn't matter how big or small they may be; show yourself some love.

_____

_____

_____

_____

_____

_____

_____

_____

_____

_____

_____

_____

_____

_____

_____

_____

_____

_____

SELF-APPLICATION | ACKNOWLEDGE II

Think of some people who show up for you in small, but big, ways. Show them some love, too. I even encourage you to reach out to them once you've written it all out.

_____

_____

_____

_____

_____

_____

_____

_____

_____

_____

_____

_____

_____

_____

_____

_____

_____

_____

Phase V
Arrival

December 2018

You're off the plane, you've stopped by the restroom to fix yourself up a bit, and you're relieved to be back on solid ground after such an unpredictable flight. The first thing you do is let those who are important to you know you've made it safely. Can you guess how I'm going to apply this to real life? If so, you get me!

Supporting people who are going through trials isn't an easy endeavor, so it's time to thank the people who stayed with you through your turbulent ride. When you come through a trying time, you notice that "the little things" are big deals. Whenever my sister would go to the store, she'd ask me if I needed something or plan fun nights in because she knew I was watching what I spent. My mom would call and check in regularly, scoop me for lunch, or go for a ride for one of those mother-daughter talks. My daddy would see to it that my car was in tip-top condition, drop off lunch money (you're never too old for lunch money), and made sure I was spiritually fed every Sunday. They never rushed me or pressed the job issue unless I wanted to talk about it.

Friends became easier to distinguish, too. Remember earlier when I mentioned the different types of friends we all have? Realistically, roles in friendships, and any relationship, may need to switch up. Since I couldn't be the check-in friend, my friends clocked in and began doing this effortlessly once I finally opened up and explained what was going on with me. How can your friends really *be* friends if you're working overtime to project togetherness? They can't! How can you expect to be understood when you don't communicate effectively (or at all)? You won't! If you have friends who genuinely show concern, let them in. It'll be a weight lifted, and a bond strengthened.

I would open text messages to words of encouragement just because. They'd call to have conversations unrelated to my job search and its accompanying frustrations. Even though they knew I wouldn't be able to attend certain get-togethers, they still included me in plans so I didn't feel left out. **Most importantly, they didn't judge me or share my vulnerabilities with other people**. That's love.

Turbulence taught me one person should never be limited to one role in your life because if so, you will always be disappointed. We are not one-dimensional beings. Give people room to be whoever they need to be for the moment without taking it personally. Sometimes the friend who always checks in needs to be checked on. Sometimes the friend who does all of the planning needs an opportunity to tap out and just be given a plan. Sometimes the friend who is always down for the turn-up needs a moment to turn down. This is true for relationships, too. I never knew how patient and encouraging my significant other could be until this time. He carried the relationship in a way that I couldn't and did it without complaint. Things like this made it easier to ignore those moments when it *seemed* like nobody noticed my fall back.

The enemy will magnify the smallest things to make them appear worse than they are. All of that social media related self-doubt was nothing compared to the quality of my circle. I now care more about those who showed up in these quiet ways, during my turbulent time, because I see that they are the ones who care about me landing in one piece. Now, it's time for the ride to your final destination.

If you're like me, you don't like a chatty Lyft driver, so you keep conversation relatively short, hoping it sends a clear message. Before you know it you're gazing out of the window, reflecting on things you hadn't thought about before. As much as I detested not working, I needed all of that unwanted downtime. When I would read articles about the importance of "finding yourself," I used to think the idea was pretty corny because I didn't get what it meant.

Who out there doesn't know who they are? I thought. What is this vague phrase everyone keeps repeating? If you're always on the move, you can't digest what this means or what it involves. My pilot was trying to signal for me to sit down and since I didn't, He sat me down. In thinking back over the years that led to my twenties, I couldn't think of a period when I wasn't working since I was sixteen.

My first job was at Chick-fil-a, and next was at Party City. In college, I had a work-study, was involved in multiple organizations, and ran the yard on campus. My line sisters and I took pride in quality programming, community service, and performances – Hey, Femme Fatales! In graduate school, I worked two jobs in addition to my full time, unpaid internship. Even during my first two years as a teacher, I had another part-time job. Have you ever looked back at a time when you did *the most* and thought, "How did I do all of that?" I needed to get somewhere and get still.

Joy came from the smallest things during those moments I spent seated. I got into YouTube tutorials and started subscribing to different beauty influencers' channels. Now, I can do my own makeup! I'd practice a few times a week whether I was going somewhere or not. My sister would come home and give me a puzzled look when she realized I had on a full face of makeup with pajamas on.

"Did you go somewhere today or...?"

"Nope," I'd respond, "just practicing."

She'd nod and say, "Oh ok" and let me be. I was going to be fine even if I was only hanging around the house. Whenever I *do* have somewhere to go, I thought, my face is going to be on point.

Remember when I said I'd purchase one thing for my wardrobe every few weeks so I'd be ready for the new chapter in my life? Discovering my personal style was pretty exciting. I started figuring out which colors work for me and which ones don't. In addition to this, I know what flatters my body type and what to avoid. After researching skin types, I finally found the perfect skincare routine for me and invested in quality products. I saw the difference and this, too, was exciting.

I forgot what it was like to get into a good show without checking my phone or email every few minutes, and now I'm into TV shows I'd been missing out on. I lost weight from my running regimen. I learned how to make a few new dishes. Reading was something I had time for again. I may not have been clocking into work, but I got up every day, opened my laptop, and worked on this book. Who knew self-care was so important?

There were so many things I didn't realize I gained from that downtime because the turbulence distorted it all. The confidence I used to get from being planned and having control of everything around me, was now coming from the inside. I mastered the art of looking and feeling good.

As awkward as it is to admit, I found myself.

SELF-APPLICATION | OWN IT

What have you realized about yourself? What are some of the key characteristics of your personality that shape who you are?

_____

_____

_____

_____

_____

_____

_____

_____

_____

_____

_____

_____

_____

_____

_____

_____

_____

Phase VI
Helping Someone Else

January 2019-

Wanderlust is real after college. My first flight was during the summer of 2015- my first summer break as a teacher. Now that I had a little bit of money I wanted to explore. Although I had a desire to leave the country, I knew I needed to take baby steps and stay within the states. I locked down on a location and packed my bags with enthusiasm. My parents gave me a red set of luggage for Christmas, and it was finally being put to good use. Since this was my first flight, I was a little apprehensive and had lots of questions about what to expect at the airport *and* in the air.

I called up a friend for an idea of what to expect at the airport because, as you know, I needed to be ready for the experience so that I could plan accordingly. To write down everything she said, I put her on speakerphone so I could type into the 'notes' application on my phone.

"Hey! I'm going to fly for the first time soon, but I don't know about all of the airport stuff. What do I need to do? Like when I get there?" I asked.

"Just make sure you have your ID and your boarding pass," she answered. "That's pretty much it to be honest with you."

It couldn't be that simple, could it?

"So wait, I walk in with my stuff, show my ID, and that's it? I thought it'd be more to it than that because I heard you need to get to the airport like two hours early. Are you sure?"

She took a deep breath. "Yes, girl. I mean you'll need to go through security and stuff, but yea that's pretty much it."

I stopped there. It sounded like my questions were annoying her, so I didn't want to press for additional details. *Just have your license and boarding pass, and go through security*, I thought to myself. Well readers, let me tell you how my first visit to the airport went down.

After being dropped off, I walked in and was surprisingly overwhelmed by the amount of movement happening around me. The lobby was teeming with people who were powerwalking to their respective service counters. Have you all seen the *Mr. Krabs* meme where he's confused, and everything around him is a blur? That was me. I eyeballed my airline and saw people standing in line, so I followed suit with my luggage, my license, and my boarding pass.

When it was my turn to step up, the attendant looked irritated, and I could tell it was because of something I hadn't done.

"Where is the tag for your bag?"

"What tag?" I asked.

I had no idea what she was talking about and to make matters worse she was obnoxiously loud, so I was embarrassed.

"Go back to one of the kiosks and print your boarding pass and tag your bag," she snapped. "Next!"

Okay, so my friend didn't tell me this.

I turned around, found an open kiosk, and followed the steps to receive a bag tag. With the help of a floating attendant who noticed me trying to read the instructions, I finally got the tag onto my bag correctly. When I walked back to the attendant at the counter, she took my bag and threw it onto the conveyer belt screaming, "Next!" This lady, who was apparently having a bad day, was in such a hurry to get to the next customer I couldn't ask her my next question. Where was the line for security?

I am officially flustered.

In an attempt to shadow someone from that point on, I hung around the area until another person walked by (somebody who looked like they knew where they were going). I stayed on some random woman's heels until we arrived at the line for security. The line was pretty long, so I decided to get on my phone to pass the time. Soon, it was my turn to step up. Unfortunately, since I was distracted the entire wait, I didn't notice anything else I needed to have ready to go.

"License and boarding pass, please."

Oh my gosh, I'd already put it up. My friend didn't tell me anything about keeping this out after checking in. I had to dig back through my carry-on bag to find them, but I didn't know which compartment they were in. I knew I was holding up the line and this irritated the officer even more.

"Please already have your license and boarding pass out, people!" he yells to everyone behind me, making it even more evident that I was unprepared. First of all, I thought, you didn't have to call me out to prove a point. Once I found them, I was cleared. I made it my business to put my phone away. I needed to be observant until I was seated on the plane.

Next, they needed to check my personal bag, and I needed to walk through the metal detector. Here, it was easy to play follow the leader because you can watch people ahead of you before it's your turn to proceed. Take off your shoes. Grab a bin. Put items in the bin. Wait in line. As you can probably guess, I still screwed it up.

I didn't know that I had to pull out all of my electronics and that bottles containing liquids had to be thrown away if they were over the three-ounce limit. Looking back, this must've been an off day because someone is always prompting travelers to remove these things. Not on this day. I tried to explain myself when I was told to trash my things, but security was not in a position to make exceptions. My unopened Fiji water and an unopened bottle of body wash were garbage. Now, I'm frustrated.

Finally, after following the crowd again, I get to the plane train. This is designed to take me to the gate listed on my boarding pass- something else I wasn't informed of. When the doors opened, there was so much congestion I practically had to push people over to get on. Rushing to make it without getting caught in the closing doors, I didn't have time to gain my bearings before the train took off and I fell. You read that right.

I fell over, catching myself with both hands like a child who has tripped mid-run on the playground. What made matters worse is it took a second for me to get up and get myself together. An elderly man looked over at me, smiling, and said, "It's pretty fast, huh?" Talk about embarrassed. Oh, so *that's* why everyone is holding onto something. Now, I'm over it.

When I asked my friend about getting through the airport, she didn't mention any of these things. This was my first time being subjected to airport procedures, and **she didn't approach our conversation with my learning curve in mind.** I wasn't informed of any of the particulars that occur between being dropped off and making it to your flight gate. There was much more to getting through than just having my boarding pass and license out, but she made it seem like this process was common sense. I recognize now why so much information was unintentionally excluded. She was a regular flier.

She'd been there and done that, so she didn't feel obligated to break things because once you're used to something you don't realize all it entails.

If someone were to ask my dad about fixing a car, he could do whatever needs to be done quicker than breaking down every detail involved. If someone were to ask my mama how to cook a particular dish, she'd need a moment to sit and think about every step to write out for you because, for her, cooking is second nature. Once we've mastered something, we aren't mindful of every factor involved and this is normal. We just do it. We cannot, however, be this general when trying to help other people in their lives, and I didn't realize this until an experience came full circle for me.

I first began mentoring by way of a summer program at the University of Tennessee, an initiative that encourages students from two target high schools to attend a post-secondary institution. Every June, my alma mater hosted a group of junior and senior students to stay on campus for a week and experience college life.

My duty was to act a "mentor." That included supervising the girls on my floor, helping them with assignments, and having candid conversations with them about they should expect once they stepped foot on a college campus. We were also told it was not uncommon for students to want to keep in touch once the summer institute was over. If we felt we could help them beyond the program, we were given the liberty to do so. I didn't think I'd do this.

Now when I applied for this mentoring position it sounded like a fun summer gig, but I didn't know what it meant to be a mentor, hence me placing quotations around the word mentor earlier. I never had one, so I figured it was like being one of those overly-enthusiastic camp counselors. As long as I remained upbeat and was accessible for questions and tutoring, I thought I was honoring that title. Little did I know, mentoring is a loaded word that requires much more than a smiling face and help with an English paper.

Traniece, a junior at the time, was my first mentee and I instantly recognized she was mature for her age. Her personality was larger than life, she was a hilariously sarcastic, very outspoken, and could read people in a heartbeat. Of course she was on my floor, and of course she was trying to leave the floor right after the coordinator told them they couldn't.

"Why not?" she asked me, as I sat next to the elevators to block the exit doors.

"Well, they just told you all you couldn't leave. You should've eaten at dinner," I responded.

I was trying to sound as pleasant as possible. I was tired from helping with move-in that day and leading some of the icebreakers that followed. The first day of any summer camp, I'm convinced, is the most demanding. Lucky for me,

I had night shift this day too, so the exhaustion was at an all-time high.

"That isn't a reason, though," she pressed.

Ugh. Why me? Why my night?

"It's late," I reminded her, "and we want you to get ready for tomorrow. You have to be up at 6:00 AM to have enough time to get ready for your first class. In college, you'll have to prioritize your time this way, too."

I thought my response would make her back down, but she still wasn't having it.

"Okay, so if this is supposed to give us a taste of what college is like, shouldn't I be able to do that and deal with being sleepy in the morning? Wouldn't that be *my* problem?" she returned.

Oh wow. She had a point-a valid one at that. She's one of *those* students. I like her!

We talked during the institute and even bickered a bit because some aspects of our

[108]

personality were identical, but when the institute was over, we exchanged information and kept in touch. As time went on, Traniece was preparing to go to college while I was finishing graduate school. My patience had grown thin with her because, as I mentioned at the beginning of the book, I was beginning to realize I wasn't doing what I wanted to do long-term. We were entering new worlds at the same time.

Her once tolerable sarcasm now felt aggravating and unnecessary because I thought she should've known better. When she'd ask me specific questions, or wanted to know the reason why something she said wasn't as tactful or appropriate as it could be, I didn't have the patience to break down the "whys." Her maturity, to me, was an indication that she was smart enough to figure it out. Just because somebody is wise beyond their years, doesn't mean they can do everything on their own, all the time.

We all need support.

How I handled Traniece was how my friend handled me when I asked about getting through the airport. I didn't make time to give her a detailed blueprint that could've helped her navigate things until later when we randomly fell back in touch. She was smart enough to figure out most of it, and I'm proud of how she's handling the things life is throwing at her, but I know I could've done more *then*. She may not have listened, but at least I would've been at peace knowing I addressed her questions in an empathetic way.

All things are intentional. We purposely lost contact for me to realize I could've handled her inquisitiveness differently. I also know that she had her own epiphanies during this period, too. Now that I have a greater understanding of this, I'm going to try my best not to miss any more opportunities with anybody. Between my awkward airport experience, and Traniece and

I's relationship coming full circle, I recognize the importance of slowing down and taking time to hear, respond, and interact with other people. This is my new mission.

When we *can* help someone else, we should. The inconvenience isn't greater than the act itself. Taking a leap of faith will do more than get you from where you are to where you want to be, but it will also school you in ways your family, friends, and even teachers cannot. The sooner you're schooled, the sooner you will be in a position to share your story and help people you never thought needed help.

This was one of the many things that I reaped from my leap of faith: a greater understanding of who I am, a greater desire to help other people, and a greater understanding of people in general. This process had less to do with getting what I wanted and more to do with how to be a better person to other people.

It's not about us.

SELF APPLICATION | WHO'S NEXT?

When is the last time you've taken the time to help someone get through a turbulent time in *their* life? If you haven't, think of some people you can help. If you have, jot it down + reflect on what you learned from that experience.

_____

_____

_____

_____

_____

_____

_____

_____

_____

_____

_____

_____

_____

_____

_____

_____

Epilogue

So about the job— As of December 2018, I'm still waiting. I know, not the typical happy ending, right? Wrong. The beauty in waiting *this* time is that I'm going to let the chips fall where they may and be okay with the result. In the meantime, I'm still "working" in other ways. A job doesn't make or break me.

Do I get frustrated? Absolutely, but I'm not going to let the idea of another delay induce doubt. I'm going to persevere because my faith is not a mistake and neither is yours.

Chesley Sullenberger isn't considered a skilled pilot because of how he handled clear skies and windless weather. He's revered for how he landed his aircraft onto the Hudson River after a flock of geese disabled its engines. Rather than panicking and losing control, he used his training and discernment to land intentionally, without a single fatality. God trains us like this.

When we ask Him for more, it's almost as if He enlists us into a spiritual flight training. This intensive experience is deliberate in that it forces us to use preexisting skills when faced with inclement weather. Rather than deciding the storm is a sign to abort the mission, He wants to see if we'll force ourselves to use everything He's giving us to land safely. Once we've made it through, we know we've not only enhanced our skill set but know we are perfectly capable of handling any storm, too. Which type of pilot are you? Will people want to ride with you during a storm, or not?

My leap of faith taught me that real transformation happens once we find beauty in our substandard situations rather than gripe about the discomfort of them. The Bible, yet again, affirms this. In Hebrews 12:1-2 it reads,

"Therefore let us also, seeing we are compassed about with so great a cloud of witnesses, <u>lay aside every weight, and the sin which doth so easily beset us, and let us run the race that is set before us, Looking unto Jesus the author and perfecter of our faith, who for the job that was set before him endured the cross, despising shame</u>, and hath sat down at the right hand of the throne of God." (KJV)

We must continuously run our races with our heads held high. Granted, this isn't easy. Sometimes we've been positive for so long that we decide we've earned the right to unleash the beast and have a negative moment because we're exhausted. Fight that urge. A dear friend of mind, Kevin, texted me checking in while I was in the beginning stages of this intensive training. All I spoke on was the fact that I was unemployed and discouraged because, at the time, there was nothing else to discuss. Or so I thought.

He responded saying, "I'm gonna ask you that "how are you?" question again in a few days, and hopefully your circumstances won't lead your answer. There's much more to this time in your life than that."

Checked, yet again. Sheesh.

I can't wait until we catch up again. He'll know that I'm in a new city, that I've just finished my first book, and that I'm looking forward to what's coming. I'm good. Once *you* decide to leap, you will be good, too. God can't move until you decide inaction is no longer an option. So, what are you waiting for?

Matthew 6:31-33

Monthly Leap Sheets

The next few pages are for you to use as an accountability tool for the year. Each month is blank so that you can decide when you're ready to start. Write down your goals, reflect on your lessons, and watch what you want gradually manifest! It's time to start working towards fulfillment.

→

MONTH #1

_____

PROFESSIONAL	PERSONAL
BODY	_____

MONTHLY REFLECTION

Of the goals listed and completed for this month,
which was the most difficult + why?

What did you learn from this difficulty?

MONTH #2

PROFESSIONAL	PERSONAL
BODY	_____

MONTHLY REFLECTION

Of the goals listed and completed for this month,
which was the most difficult + why?

What did you learn from this difficulty?

MONTH #3

_____

PROFESSIONAL	PERSONAL
BODY	_____

MONTHLY REFLECTION

Of the goals listed and completed for this month, which was the most difficult + why?

What did you learn from this difficulty?

MONTH #4

PROFESSIONAL	PERSONAL
BODY	_____

MONTHLY REFLECTION

Of the goals listed and completed for this month, which was the most difficult + why?

What did you learn from this difficulty?

MONTH #5

PROFESSIONAL	PERSONAL
BODY	_____

MONTHLY REFLECTION

Of the goals listed and completed for this month, which was the most difficult + why?

What did you learn from this difficulty?

MONTH #6- HALFWAY THERE ☺

PROFESSIONAL	PERSONAL

BODY	_____

MONTHLY REFLECTION

Of the goals listed and completed for this month, which was the most difficult + why?

What did you learn from this difficulty?

MONTH #7

_____

PROFESSIONAL	PERSONAL
BODY	_____

MONTHLY REFLECTION

Of the goals listed and completed for this month, which was the most difficult + why?

What did you learn from this difficulty?

MONTH #8

PROFESSIONAL

PERSONAL

BODY

MONTHLY REFLECTION

Of the goals listed and completed for this month, which was the most difficult + why?

What did you learn from this difficulty?

MONTH #9

_____

PROFESSIONAL	PERSONAL
BODY	_____

MONTHLY REFLECTION

Of the goals listed and completed for this month, which was the most difficult + why?

What did you learn from this difficulty?

MONTH #10

PROFESSIONAL	PERSONAL
BODY	_____

MONTHLY REFLECTION

Of the goals listed and completed for this month, which was the most difficult + why?

What did you learn from this difficulty?

MONTH #11

PROFESSIONAL	PERSONAL
BODY	_____

MONTHLY REFLECTION

Of the goals listed and completed for this month, which was the most difficult + why?

What did you learn from this difficulty?

YOU'RE FINISHING STRONG! I SEE YOU!

PROFESSIONAL	PERSONAL

BODY	_____

MONTHLY REFLECTION

Of the goals listed and completed for this month, which was the most difficult + why?

What did you learn from this difficulty?

CONGRATULATIONS

YOU DID IT!

If you've made it here, you're the G.O.A.T! It takes discipline to actively work towards your goals when no one is watching. I dare you to do it again every year. Identify your biggest takeaways from this year and use them to your advantage as you move forward. Who knows, I could be reading YOUR book next!

The best thing that happened this year was:

_____

_____

_____

One things I wish I could've done differently is:

_____

_____

_____

Moving forward, I'm going to:

_____

_____

_____

→

Connect with KG

Instagram: _25karats

I'd love to hear about your journey
or your testimony.

32175864R00086

Made in the USA
Middletown, DE
04 January 2019